Homemade Protein Shakes for Maximum Muscle Growth:

Change Your Body without Pills or Creatine Supplements

By

Joseph Correa

Certified Sports Nutritionist

COPYRIGHT

© 2015 Correa Media Group

All rights reserved

Reproduction or translation of any part of this work beyond that permitted by section 107 or 108 of the 1976 United States Copyright Act without the permission of the copyright owner is unlawful.

This publication is designed to provide accurate and authoritative information in regard to

The subject matter covered. It is sold with the understanding that neither the author nor the publisher is engaged in rendering medical advice. If medical advice or assistance is needed, consult with a doctor. This book is considered a guide and should not be used in any way detrimental to your health. Consult with a physician before starting this nutritional plan to make sure it's right for you.

ACKNOWLEDGEMENTS

The realization and success of this book could not have been possible without my family.

Homemade Protein Shakes for Maximum Muscle Growth:

Change Your Body without Pills or Creatine Supplements

By

Joseph Correa

Certified Sports Nutritionist

CONTENTS

Copyright

Acknowledgements

About The Author

Introduction

Homemade Protein Shakes for Maximum Muscle Growth

Other Great Titles by This Author

ABOUT THE AUTHOR

As a certified sports nutritionist and professional athlete, I firmly believe that proper nutrition will help you reach your goals faster and effectively. My knowledge and experience has helped me live healthier throughout the years and which I have shared with family and friends. The more you know about eating and drinking healthier, the sooner you will want to change your life and eating habits.

Being successful in controlling your weight is important as it will improve all aspects of your life.

Nutrition is a key part in the process of getting in better shape and that's what this book is all about.

INTRODUCTION

Homemade Protein Shakes for Maximum Muscle Growth: Change Your Body without Pills or Creatine Supplements

This book will help you increase the amount of protein you consume per day to help increase muscle mass. These meals will help increase muscle in an organized manner by adding large healthy portions of protein to your diet. Being too busy to eat right can sometimes become a problem and that's why this book will save you time and help nourish your body to achieve the goals you want. Make sure you know what you're eating by preparing it yourself or having someone prepare it for you.

This book will help you to:

-Gain muscle fast naturally.

-Improve muscle recovery.

-Have more energy.

-Naturally accelerate Your Metabolism to build more muscle.

-Improve your digestive system.

Joseph Correa is a certified sports nutritionist and a professional athlete.

HOMEMADE PROTEIN SHAKES FOR MAXIMUM MUSCLE GROWTH

1. Oat & Almond Shake

Preparing time: 5 minutes
Servings: 3

1. *Ingredients:*

220ml milk
1 tablespoon almonds (grinded) (15g)
1 tablespoon oats (15g)
1 teaspoon maple syrup (5g)
½ teaspoon vanilla extract (2-3g)
2 tablespoon Greek Yogurt (30g)
30g whey protein

2. *Preparation:*

All ingredients go in a blender and are blend until the consistence is smooth.

3. *Nutritional facts (amount per 100ml/entire composition):*

Contains calcium, iron;

Calories: 111	Total Fat: 3.2g
Calories from Fat: 29	Saturated Fat: 0.7g

Cholesterol: 21mg
Sodium: 58mg

Potassium: 182mg

Total Carbohydrates: 9.3g
    Dietary Fiber: 0.8g
    Sugar: 5.1g
Protein: 11.1g
Calories: 333

    Calories from Fat: 86

Total Fat: 9.5g

Saturated Fat: 2.1g

Cholesterol: 64mg

Sodium: 175mg

Potassium: 547mg

Total Carbohydrates: 27.9g
    Dietary Fiber: 2.6g
    Sugar: 15.3g
Protein: 33.5g

2. Peppermint Oatmeal Shake

Preparing time: 5 minutes
Servings: 5

1. Ingredients:

70g oatmeal
30g bran flakes
300ml milk
50g quark
½ teaspoon peppermint extract (3g)
30g ice-cream (vanilla/chocolate)
50g whey protein (chocolate)

2. Preparation:

Mix all ingredients in a blender until the composition is smooth.

3. Nutritional facts (amount per 100ml/entire composition):

Contains Vitamin A, calcium, iron.

Calories: 180
    Calories from Fat: 51

Total Fat: 5.6g
    Saturated Fat: 2.9g

Cholesterol: 30mg
Sodium: 111mg

Potassium: 179mg

Total Carbohydrates: 20.7g
    Dietary Fiber: 2.5g
    Sugar: 6.2g
Protein: 12.6g
Calories: 900

Homemade Protein Shakes for Maximum Muscle Growth

Calories from Fat: 253

Total Fat: 28.1g

   Saturated Fat: 14.4g

Cholesterol: 151mg

Sodium: 555mg

Potassium: 869mg

Total Carbohydrates: 104g
   Dietary Fiber: 12.4g
   Sugar: 31.2g

Protein: 63.2g

3. Cinnamon Shake

Preparing time: 5 minutes
Servings: 3

1. Ingredients:

240ml milk
¼ tablespoon cinnamon (4g)
½ teaspoon vanilla extracts (3g)
2 tablespoon vanilla ice-cream (30g)
2 tablespoon oats (30g)
50g whey protein

2. Preparation:

Mix all ingredients in a blender until the composition is smooth.

3. Nutritional facts (amount per 100g/entire composition):

Contains Vitamin A, calcium, iron.

Calories: 131
    Calories from Fat: 30

Total Fat: 3.3g
    Saturated Fat: 1.8g

Cholesterol: 42mg
Sodium: 73mg

Potassium: 158mg

Total Carbohydrates: 10.3g
    Dietary Fiber: 1g
    Sugar: 4.8g
Protein: 15.3g

Calories: 342

    Calories from Fat: 89

Total Fat: 9.9g

Saturated Fat: 5.4g

Cholesterol: 127mg

Sodium: 219mg

Potassium: 474mg

Total Carbohydrates: 31g
   Dietary Fiber: 3.1g
   Sugar: 14.4g
Protein: 45.9g

4. Almonds Shake

Preparing time: 5 minutes
Servings: 5

1. Ingredients:

220ml almond milk
120g oatmeal
50g whey protein
80g raisins
20g almonds (grinded)
1 tablespoon peanut butter (15g)

2. Preparation:

Mix all ingredients in a blender until the composition is smooth.

3. Nutritional facts (amount per 100g/entire composition):

Contains : Vitamin C, iron, calcium.

Calories: 241
    Calories from Fat: 61

Total Fat: 6.7g
    Saturated Fat: 1.6g

Cholesterol: 24mg
Sodium: 57mg

Potassium: 339mg

Total Carbohydrates: 33.8g
    Dietary Fiber: 3.7g
    Sugar: 12.5g
Protein: 13.9g

Calories: 1207
    Calories from Fat: 304

Total Fat: 33.7g

Saturated Fat: 8g

Cholesterol: 122mg

Sodium: 283mg

Potassium: 1693mg

Total Carbohydrates: 169g
   Dietary Fiber: 18.5g
   Sugar: 62.3g
Protein: 69.4g

5. Banana & Almonds Shake

Preparing time: 5 minutes
Servings: 5

1. Ingredients:

2 bananas
230ml almond milk
20g almonds (grinded)
10g pistachios (grinded)
40g whey protein

2. Preparation:

Mix all ingredients in a blender until the composition is smooth.

3. Nutritional facts (amount per 100g/entire composition):

Contains Vitamin A, C, iron, calcium.

Calories: 241
    Calories from Fat: 61

Total Fat: 6.7g
    Saturated Fat: 1.6g

Cholesterol: 24mg
Sodium: 57mg

Potassium: 339mg

Total Carbohydrates: 33.8g
    Dietary Fiber: 3.7g
    Sugar: 12.5g
Protein: 13.9g

Calories: 1073

    Calories from Fat: 659

Total Fat: 73.2g

Saturated Fat: 52.1g

Cholesterol: 83mg

Sodium: 109mg

Potassium: 1934mg

Total Carbohydrates: 78.7g
- Dietary Fiber: 14.8g
- Sugar: 39.4g

Protein: 42.8g

6. Wild Berry Shake

Preparing time: 5 minutes
Servings: 7

1. Ingredients:

30g strawberries
30g blueberries
30g raspberries
30g currants
500ml milk
60g whey protein
1 teaspoon vanilla extract (5g)
1 teaspoon lemon extract (5g)

2. Preparation:

Mix all ingredients in a blender until the composition is smooth. You can also add some ice cubes to the mix.

3. Nutritional facts (amount per 100g/entire composition):

Contains Vitamin A, C, iron, calcium.

Calories: 78
    Calories from Fat: 19

Total Fat: 2.1g
    Saturated Fat: 1.2g

Cholesterol: 24mg
Sodium: 50mg

Potassium: 119mg

Total Carbohydrates: 6.7g
    Dietary Fiber: 0.7g
    Sugar: 4.7g
Protein: 8.7g
Calories: 549

Calories from Fat: 131

Total Fat: 14.6g

   Saturated Fat: 8.1g

Cholesterol: 167mg

Sodium: 351mg

Potassium: 832mg

Total Carbohydrates: 46.9g

   Dietary Fiber: 4.6g

   Sugar: 33g

Protein: 61g

7. Strawberry Shake

Preparing time: 5 minutes
Servings: 5

1. Ingredients:

30g strawberries
100g Greek Yogurt
200ml milk
40g whey protein
2 eggs
20g sweetener (honey/ brown sugar)
ice cubes
1 teaspoon vanilla extract (5g)

2. Preparation:

Mix all ingredients in a blender until the composition is smooth.

The Greek Yogurt can have different aromas like vanilla or strawberry, or just be plain yogurt. It works will all flavors.

3. Nutritional facts (amount per 100g/entire composition):

Contains Vitamin A, C, iron, calcium.

Calories: 96	Cholesterol: 87mg
Calories from Fat: 32	Sodium: 65mg
Total Fat: 3.5g	Potassium: 131mg
Saturated Fat: 1.6g	

Homemade Protein Shakes for Maximum Muscle Growth

Total Carbohydrates: 9.2g
    Dietary Fiber: 2.5g
    Sugar: 3.4g
Protein: 11.3g

Calories: 508

    Calories from Fat: 157

Total Fat: 17.4g

    Saturated Fat: 8g

Cholesterol: 433mg

Sodium: 326mg

Potassium: 656mg

Total Carbohydrates: 45.9g
    Dietary Fiber: 12.4g
    Sugar: 17.2g
Protein: 56.6g

8. Strawberry Vanilla Shake

Preparing time: 5 minutes
Servings: 7

1. Ingredients:

100g strawberries
1 banana
1 teaspoon vanilla extract (5g)
1 tablespoon strawberries extract (15g)
50g oats
200ml milk
5 eggs
Ice cubes

2. Preparation:

Mix all ingredients in a blender until the composition is smooth.

3. Nutritional facts (amount per 100g/entire composition):

Contains Vitamin A, C, iron, calcium.

Calories: 112
    Calories from Fat: 39

Total Fat: 4.3g
    Saturated Fat: 1.4g

Cholesterol: 119mg
Sodium: 59mg

Potassium: 170mg

Total Carbohydrates: 11.7g
    Dietary Fiber: 1.4g
    Sugar: 4.6g
Protein: 6.1g

Calories: 782

    Calories from Fat: 271

Total Fat: 30.1g

    Saturated Fat: 10.1g

Cholesterol: 835mg

Sodium: 421mg

Potassium: 1189mg

Total Carbohydrates: 82g
    Dietary Fiber: 10.1g
    Sugar: 32.5g

Protein: 43g

9. Strawberry & Nuts Shake

Preparing time: 5 minutes
Servings: 4

1. Ingredients:

50g strawberries
50g mix nuts (chopped)
200ml milk
100g Greek yogurt
2 tablespoon oats (30g)

2. Preparation:

Mix all ingredients in a blender until the composition is smooth.

3. Nutritional facts (amount per 100g/entire composition):

Contains Vitamin A, C, iron, calcium.

Calories: 140
    Calories from Fat: 81

Total Fat: 9g
    Saturated Fat: 1.4g

Cholesterol: 1mg
Sodium: 80mg

Potassium: 125mg

Total Carbohydrates: 9.2g
    Dietary Fiber: 1.4g
    Sugar: 4.3g
Protein: 6.9g
Calories: 417

    Calories from Fat: 324

Total Fat: 36g

    Saturated Fat: 5.4g

Cholesterol: 5mg

Sodium: 321mg

Potassium: 499mg

Total Carbohydrates: 36.9g
Dietary Fiber: 5.5g
Sugar: 17.1g
Protein: 27.6g

10. Raspberry Shake

Preparing time: 5 minutes
Servings: 4

1. Ingredients:

50g whey protein
100g raspberries
30g strawberries
50g sour cream
200ml milk
1 teaspoon lime extract (5g)

2. Preparation:

Mix all ingredients in a blender until the composition is smooth.

3. Nutritional facts (amount per 100g/entire composition):

Contains Vitamin A, C, B-12, iron, calcium.

Calories: 116
    Calories from Fat: 41

Total Fat: 4.6g
    Saturated Fat: 2.6g

Cholesterol: 36mg
Sodium: 54mg

Potassium: 168mg

Total Carbohydrates: 8.1g
    Dietary Fiber: 1.8g
    Sugar: 4.2g
Protein: 11.4g
Calories: 465

    Calories from Fat: 166

Total Fat: 18.4g

Saturated Fat: 10.6g

Cholesterol: 143mg

Sodium: 214mg

Potassium: 670mg

Total Carbohydrates: 32.5g
Dietary Fiber: 7.1g
Sugar: 16.8g
Protein: 45.5g

11. Blueberry Shake

Preparing time: 5 minutes
Servings: 6

1. Ingredients:

250g blueberries
50g sour cream
80g oats
100ml coconut milk
160g pumpkin puree
Cinnamon, nutmeg for sprinkle on top

2. Preparation:

Mix all ingredients in a blender until the composition is smooth.

3. Nutritional facts (amount per 100g/entire composition):

Contains Vitamin A, C, iron, calcium.

Calories: 140
    Calories from Fat: 62

Total Fat: 6.9g
    Saturated Fat: 4.8g

Cholesterol: 4mg
Sodium: 9mg

Potassium: 192mg

Total Carbohydrates: 18.5g
    Dietary Fiber: 3.5g
    Sugar: 5.7g
Protein: 3g
Calories: 641

    Calories from Fat: 371

Total Fat: 41.2g

Saturated Fat: 29.1g

Cholesterol: 22mg

Sodium: 56mg

Potassium: 1150mg

Total Carbohydrates: 112g
Dietary Fiber: 21g
Sugar: 34.4g
Protein: 18.1g

12. Peanut Butter Shake

Preparing time: 5 minutes
Servings: 6

1. Ingredients:

300ml almond milk
50g peanut butter
50g mix nuts
6 egg whites
1 teaspoon butter extract (5g)

2. Preparation:

Mix all ingredients in a blender until the composition is smooth.

3. Nutritional facts (amount per 100g/entire composition):

Contains Vitamin C, iron, calcium.

Calories: 236
    Calories from Fat: 191

Total Fat: 21.3g
    Saturated Fat: 12.2g

Cholesterol: 0mg
Sodium: 109mg

Potassium: 241mg

Total Carbohydrates: 6.2g
    Dietary Fiber: 2g
    Sugar: 3.1g
Protein: 8.3g
Calories: 1415

    Calories from Fat: 1148

Total Fat: 127.6g

Saturated Fat: 73.1g

Cholesterol: 0mg

Sodium: 656mg

Potassium: 1448mg

Total Carbohydrates: 37.2g
Dietary Fiber: 11.9g
Sugar: 18.5g
Protein: 50.2g

13. Peanut Butter & Banana Shake

Preparing time: 5 minutes
Servings: 7

1. Ingredients:

250ml almond milk
2 bananas
30g peanut butter
5 eggs
2 teaspoons honey (10g)
1 teaspoon vanilla extract (5g)

2. Preparation:

Mix all ingredients in a blender until the composition is smooth.

3. Nutritional facts (amount per 100g/entire composition):

Contains Vitamin A, C, iron, calcium.

Calories: 191
    Calories from Fat: 126

Total Fat: 14g
    Saturated Fat: 9.1g

Cholesterol: 117mg
Sodium: 70mg

Potassium: 288mg

Total Carbohydrates: 12.5g
    Dietary Fiber: 1.9g
    Sugar: 7.7g
Protein: 6.2g

Calories: 1339
    Calories from Fat: 884

Total Fat: 98.2g

Saturated Fat: 63.9g

Cholesterol: 818mg

Sodium: 487mg

Potassium: 2015mg

Total Carbohydrates: 87.6g
Dietary Fiber: 13.5g
Sugar: 53.9g
Protein: 43.6g

14. Peanut Butter & Chocolate Shake

Preparing time: 5 minutes
Servings: 3

1. Ingredients:

2 tablespoon cocoa powder (30g)
30g peanut butter
250ml almond milk
50g whey protein

2. Preparation:

Mix all ingredients in a blender until the composition is smooth.

3. Nutritional facts (amount per 100g/entire composition):

Contains Vitamin C, iron, calcium.

Calories: 326
    Calories from Fat: 240

Total Fat: 26.6g
    Saturated Fat: 19.7g

Cholesterol: 35mg
Sodium: 89mg

Potassium: 472mg

Total Carbohydrates: 10.6g
    Dietary Fiber: 3.5g
    Sugar: 4.3g
Protein: 17g
Calories: 977

    Calories from Fat: 719

Total Fat: 79.9g

    Saturated Fat: 59.1g

Cholesterol: 104mg

Sodium: 267mg

Potassium: 1415mg

Total Carbohydrates: 31.8g
Dietary Fiber: 10.6g
Sugar: 13g
Protein: 51g

15. Chocolate Shake

Preparing time: 5 minutes
Servings: 6

1. Ingredients:

3 tablespoon cocoa powder (45g)
250ml milk
120ml pumpkin puree
1 teaspoon vanilla extract (5g)
5 eggs

2. Preparation:

Mix all ingredients in a blender until the composition is smooth.

3. Nutritional facts (amount per 100g/entire composition):

Contains Vitamin A, C, iron, calcium

Calories: 89

Calories from Fat: 44

Total Fat: 4.9g

Saturated Fat: 1.9g

Cholesterol: 140mg

Sodium: 73mg

Potassium: 185mg

Total Carbohydrates: 5.6g
Dietary Fiber: 1.4g
Sugar: 3g
Protein: 6.7g
Calories: 534

Calories from Fat: 267

Total Fat: 29.6g

Saturated Fat: 11.4g

Cholesterol: 840mg

Sodium: 439mg

Potassium: 1112mg

Total Carbohydrates: 33.8g
Dietary Fiber: 8.4g
Sugar: 18.2g
Protein: 40.4g

16. Chocolate & Almond

Preparing time: 5 minutes
Servings: 5

1. Ingredients:

2 tablespoon chocolate pudding (30g)
50g almond (chopped)
300ml milk
40g whey protein
1 teaspoon amaretto syrup (5g)

2. Preparation:

Mix all ingredients in a blender until the composition is smooth.

3. Nutritional facts (amount per 100g/entire composition):

Contains Vitamin A, iron, calcium.

Calories: 131	Potassium: 154mg
Calories from Fat: 61	Total Carbohydrates: 9g
Total Fat: 6.8g	Dietary Fiber: 1.3g
	Sugar: 3.5g
Saturated Fat: 1.4g	Protein: 9.9g
	Calories: 656
Cholesterol: 22mg	
	Calories from Fat: 303
Sodium: 70mg	
	Total Fat: 33.7g

Saturated Fat: 6.9g

Cholesterol: 109mg

Sodium: 351mg

Potassium: 770mg

Total Carbohydrates: 45.2g

Dietary Fiber: 6.5g

Sugar: 17.2g

Protein: 49.3g

17. Caramel and Hazelnuts Shake

Preparing time: 5 minutes
Servings: 4

1. Ingredients:

50g hazelnuts (chopped)
1 teaspoon caramel syrup (5g)
1 teaspoon maple syrup (5g)
250ml almond milk
50g whey protein

2. Preparation:

Mix all ingredients in a blender until the composition is smooth.

3. Nutritional facts (amount per 100g/entire composition):

Contains Vitamin C, iron, calcium.

Calories: 307

Calories from Fat: 211

Total Fat: 23.4g

Saturated Fat: 14.3g

Cholesterol: 26mg

Sodium: 37mg

Potassium: 326mg

Total Carbohydrates: 15.5g
Dietary Fiber: 2.6g
Sugar: 11g
Protein: 12.2g
Calories: 1228

Calories from Fat: 844

Total Fat: 93.8g

Saturated Fat: 57.3g

Cholesterol: 104mg

Sodium: 148mg

Potassium: 1303mg

Total Carbohydrates: 61.8g
Dietary Fiber: 10.4g
Sugar: 44.1g
Protein: 49g

18. Plum Shake

Preparing time: 5 minutes
Servings: 8

1. Ingredients:

200g plum
50g raisin
200ml milk
4 eggs
100g quark
70g oats

2. Preparation:

Mix all ingredients in a blender until the composition is smooth.

3. Nutritional facts (amount per 100g/entire composition):

Contains Vitamin A, C, iron, calcium.

Calories: 122	Potassium: 149mg
Calories from Fat: 43	Total Carbohydrates: 14.7g
Total Fat: 4.7g	Dietary Fiber: 1.3g
Saturated Fat: 1.8g	Sugar: 7.2g
	Protein: 6.2g
Cholesterol: 87mg	Calories: 975
Sodium: 62mg	Calories from Fat: 340

Homemade Protein Shakes for Maximum Muscle Growth

Total Fat: 37.8g

    Saturated Fat: 14.3g

Cholesterol: 699mg

Sodium: 499mg

Potassium: 1190mg

Total Carbohydrates: 117g
    Dietary Fiber: 10.7g
    Sugar: 57.7g
Protein: 49.7g

19. Tropical Shake

Preparing time: 5 minutes
Servings: 5

1. Ingredients:

1 banana
150g pineapple
40g mango
200ml coconut milk
1 teaspoon honey (5g)
50g whey protein

2. Preparation:

Mix all ingredients in a blender until the composition is smooth.

3. Nutritional facts (amount per 100g/entire composition):

Contains Vitamin A, C, iron, calcium.

Calories: 178

Calories from Fat: 94

Total Fat: 10.4g

Saturated Fat: 8.9g

Cholesterol: 21mg

Sodium: 25mg

Potassium: 294mg

Total Carbohydrates: 15.3g

Dietary Fiber: 2.1g

Sugar: 9.9g

Protein: 8.5g

Calories: 889

Calories from Fat: 468

Total Fat: 52g

    Saturated Fat: 44.6g

Cholesterol: 104mg

Sodium: 124mg

Potassium: 1468mg

Total Carbohydrates: 76.4g
Dietary Fiber: 10.3g
Sugar: 49.2g
Protein: 42.7g

20. Peach Shake

Preparing time: 5 minutes
Servings: 8

1. Ingredients:

6 peaches
300ml milk
140g mandarins
30g oats
4 eggs

2. Preparation:

Mix all ingredients in a blender until the composition is smooth.

3. Nutritional facts (amount per 100g/entire composition):

Contains Vitamin A, C, iron, calcium.

Calories: 70

Calories from Fat: 20

Total Fat: 2.3g

Saturated Fat: 0.3g

Cholesterol: 57mg

Sodium: 34mg

Potassium: 137mg

Total Carbohydrates: 9.5g
Dietary Fiber: 1g
Sugar: 7.2g

Protein: 3.5g
Calories: 839

Calories from Fat: 245

Total Fat: 27.3g

Saturated Fat: 9.7g

Cholesterol: 680mg

Sodium: 405mg

Potassium: 1639mg

Total Carbohydrates: 115g
Dietary Fiber: 12.4g
Sugar: 86.2g
Protein: 41.6g

21. Plum & Lemon Shake

Preparing time: 5 minutes
Servings: 6

1. Ingredients:

150g plums
2 lemons (juice)
2 teaspoons honey (10g)
200ml milk
Ice cubes
150g Greek Yogurt
4 eggs

2. Preparation:

Mix all ingredients in a blender until the composition is smooth.

3. Nutritional facts (amount per 100g/entire composition):

Contains Vitamin A, C, iron, calcium.

Calories: 74	Cholesterol: 85mg
Calories from Fat: 29	Sodium: 50mg
Total Fat: 3.2g	Potassium: 111mg
Saturated Fat: 1.3g	Total Carbohydrates: 6.4g
	Dietary Fiber: 0.6g

Sugar: 5.1g
Protein: 5.8g
Calories: 589

Calories from Fat: 228

Total Fat: 25.3g

Saturated Fat: 10.3g

Cholesterol: 679mg

Sodium: 397mg

Potassium: 890mg

Total Carbohydrates: 51.2g
Dietary Fiber: 4.6g
Sugar: 40.9g
Protein: 45.9g

22. Pineapple Shake

Preparing time: 5 minutes
Servings: 6

1. Ingredients:

300g pineapple
200ml almond milk
30g raspberries
30g oats
1 lime (juice)
40g whey protein

2. Preparation:

Mix all ingredients in a blender until the composition is smooth.

3. Nutritional facts (amount per 100g/entire composition):

Contains Vitamin A, C, iron, calcium.

Calories: 153	Potassium: 218mg
Calories from Fat: 80	Total Carbohydrates: 14.4g
Total Fat: 8.9g	Dietary Fiber: 2.6g
Saturated Fat: 7.4g	Sugar: 6.7g
	Protein: 6.6g
Cholesterol: 14mg	Calories: 920
Sodium: 18mg	Calories from Fat: 481

Homemade Protein Shakes for Maximum Muscle Growth

Total Fat: 53.4g

    Saturated Fat: 44.5g

Cholesterol: 83mg

Sodium: 109mg

Potassium: 1309mg

Total Carbohydrates: 86.3g
    Dietary Fiber: 15.5g
    Sugar: 40.3g
Protein: 39.6g

23. Orange Shake

Preparing time: 5 minutes
Servings: 8

1. Ingredients:

5 oranges
10 eggs
2 tablespoon honey

2. Preparation:

Mix all ingredients in a blender until the composition is smooth.

3. Nutritional facts (amount per 100g/entire composition):

Contains Vitamin A, C, iron, calcium.

Calories: 85

Calories from Fat: 29

Total Fat: 3.2g

Saturated Fat: 1g

Cholesterol: 117mg

Sodium: 44mg

Potassium: 163mg

Total Carbohydrates: 10.4g
Dietary Fiber: 1.6g
Sugar: 8.8g
Protein: 4.6g
Calories: 1189

Calories from Fat: 404

Total Fat: 44.8g

Saturated Fat: 13.8g

Cholesterol: 1637mg

Sodium: 618mg

Potassium: 2277mg

Total Carbohydrates: 146g
Dietary Fiber: 22.2g
Sugar: 123.9g
Protein: 64.1g

24. Pinna Colada Shake

Preparing time: 5 minutes
Servings: 8

1. Ingredients:

200g pineapple
200g coconut milk
50g oats
300ml milk
4 eggs

2. Preparation:

Mix all ingredients in a blender until the composition is smooth.

3. Nutritional facts (amount per 100g/entire composition):

Contains Vitamin A, C, iron, calcium.

Calories: 128	Potassium: 149mg
Calories from Fat: 75	Total Carbohydrates: 9.8g
	Dietary Fiber: 1.1g
Total Fat: 8.3g	Sugar: 4.7g
Saturated Fat: 5.8g	Protein: 4.9g
	Calories: 1155
Cholesterol: 76mg	Calories from Fat: 675
Sodium: 48mg	Total Fat: 75g

Saturated Fat: 52.1g

Cholesterol: 680mg

Sodium: 428mg

Potassium: 1339mg

Total Carbohydrates: 87.8g
Dietary Fiber: 12.2g
Sugar: 42.2g
Protein: 44.5g

25. Apple Shake

Preparing time: 5 minutes
Servings: 3

1. Ingredients:

350g apple
1 teaspoon cinnamon
200ml almond milk
2 teaspoon vanilla extract
40g whey protein

2. Preparation:

Mix all ingredients in a blender until the composition is smooth.

3. Nutritional facts (amount per 100g/entire composition):

Contains Vitamin C, iron, calcium.

Calories: 139

Calories from Fat: 77

Total Fat: 8.6g

Saturated Fat: 7.4g

Cholesterol: 14mg

Sodium: 18mg

Potassium: 193mg

Total Carbohydrates: 11.2g
Dietary Fiber: 2.3g
Sugar: 7.6g
Protein: 5.7g
Calories: 833

Calories from Fat: 463

Total Fat: 51.4g

　Saturated Fat: 44.1g

Cholesterol: 83mg

Sodium: 106mg

Potassium: 1157mg

Total Carbohydrates: 67.3g
　Dietary Fiber: 14.2g
　Sugar: 45.5g
Protein: 34.3g

26. Egg Shake

Preparing time: 5 minutes
Servings: 8

1. Ingredients:

10 eggs
300ml milk
100g Greek Yogurt
2 tablespoon honey (30g)
50g oats

2. Preparation:

Mix all ingredients in a blender until the composition is smooth.

3. Nutritional facts (amount per 100g/entire composition):

Contains Vitamin A, iron, calcium.

Calories: 131

Calories from Fat: 55

Total Fat: 6.1g

Saturated Fat: 2.2g

Cholesterol: 185mg

Sodium: 89mg

Potassium: 123mg

Total Carbohydrates: 10.1g
Dietary Fiber: 0.6g
Sugar: 6.3g
Protein: 9.1g
Calories: 1176

Calories from Fat: 498

Homemade Protein Shakes for Maximum Muscle Growth

Total Fat: 55.3g

    Saturated Fat: 19.5g

Cholesterol: 1667mg

Sodium: 799mg

Potassium: 1111mg

Total Carbohydrates: 91.1g
    Dietary Fiber: 5.1g
    Sugar: 56.3g
Protein: 82.2g

27. Pumpkin Shake

Preparing time: 5 minutes
Servings: 6

1. Ingredients:

300g pumpkin
300g raspberries
50g sour cream
200ml almond milk
40g whey protein

2. Preparation:

Mix all ingredients in a blender until the composition is smooth.

3. Nutritional facts (amount per 100g/entire composition):

Contains Vitamin A, C, iron, calcium.

Calories: 123

Calories from Fat: 72

Total Fat: 8g

Saturated Fat: 6.4g

Cholesterol: 13mg

Sodium: 18mg

Potassium: 238mg

Total Carbohydrates: 9.8g
Dietary Fiber: 4.1g
Sugar: 3.9g

Protein: 5.2g
Calories: 986

Calories from Fat: 576

Total Fat: 64g

Saturated Fat: 51.1g

Cholesterol: 105mg

Sodium: 146mg

Potassium: 1903mg

Total Carbohydrates: 78.2g
Dietary Fiber: 32.7g
Sugar: 31.2g
Protein: 41.7g

28. Beets Shake

Preparing time: 5 minutes
Servings: 6

1. Ingredients:

300g beets
50g parsley
80g blueberries
200ml milk
60g whey protein

2. Preparation:

Mix all ingredients in a blender until the composition is smooth.

3. Nutritional facts (amount per 100g/entire composition):

Contains Vitamin A, C, iron, calcium.

Calories: 89

Calories from Fat: 14

Total Fat: 1.5g

Saturated Fat: 0.7g

Cholesterol: 24mg

Sodium: 77mg

Potassium: 285mg

Total Carbohydrates: 10.3g
Dietary Fiber: 1.6g
Sugar: 7.2g
Protein: 9.5g
Calories: 531

Calories from Fat: 81

Homemade Protein Shakes for Maximum Muscle Growth

Total Fat: 9g

    Saturated Fat: 4.5g

Cholesterol: 142mg

Sodium: 464mg

Potassium: 1711mg

Total Carbohydrates: 61.9g
Dietary Fiber: 9.6g
Sugar: 43.3g
Protein: 56.8g

29. Coconut Shake

Preparing time: 5 minutes
Servings: 5

1. Ingredients:

100ml coconut milk
200ml milk
100g Greek Yogurt
50g whey protein
1 teaspoon coconut extract
30g coconut flakes

2. Preparation:

Mix all ingredients in a blender until the composition is smooth.

3. Nutritional facts (amount per 100g/entire composition):

Contains Vitamin A, C, iron, calcium.

Calories: 145	Potassium: 184mg
Calories from Fat: 78	Total Carbohydrates: 6.2g
	Dietary Fiber: 1g
Total Fat: 8.7g	Sugar: 4.1g
Saturated Fat: 7.2g	Protein: 11.1g
	Calories: 723
Cholesterol: 25mg	
	Calories from Fat: 391
Sodium: 48mg	

Total Fat: 43.4g

Saturated Fat: 35.9g

Cholesterol: 126mg

Sodium: 241mg

Potassium: 922mg

Total Carbohydrates: 30.8g
Dietary Fiber: 4.9g
Sugar: 20.6g
Protein: 55.8g

30. Mango Shake

Preparing time: 5 minutes
Servings: 8

1. Ingredients:

3 mango fruits
1 banana
50g strawberries
300ml milk
1 lime juice
6 eggs

2. Preparation:

Mix all ingredients in a blender until the composition is smooth.

3. Nutritional facts (amount per 100g/entire composition):

Contains Vitamin A, C, iron, calcium.

Calories: 87
Calories from Fat: 31
Total Fat: 3.4g
Saturated Fat: 1.2g
Cholesterol: 101mg
Sodium: 52mg

Potassium: 155mg
Total Carbohydrates: 10.3g
Dietary Fiber: 1g
Sugar: 7.8g
Protein: 4.7g
Calories: 874
Calories from Fat: 306

Homemade Protein Shakes for Maximum Muscle Growth

Total Fat: 34g

    Saturated Fat: 12.3g

Cholesterol: 1007mg

Sodium: 524mg

Potassium: 1549mg

Total Carbohydrates: 103g
    Dietary Fiber: 9.7g
    Sugar: 78.5g
Protein: 46.7g

31. Watermelon Shake

Preparing time: 5 minutes
Servings: 6

1. Ingredients:

300g watermelon
200g cantaloupe
200ml water
1 teaspoon vanillas extract
50g sour cream
50g whey protein

2. Preparation:

Mix all ingredients in a blender until the composition is smooth.

3. Nutritional facts (amount per 100g/entire composition):

Contains Vitamin A, C, iron, calcium.

Calories: 59	Potassium: 154mg
Calories from Fat: 16	Total Carbohydrates: 5.9g
	Dietary Fiber: 0g
Total Fat: 1.8g	Sugar: 4.5g
	Protein: 5.1g
Saturated Fat: 1g	
Cholesterol: 16mg	Calories: 471
Sodium: 20mg	Calories from Fat: 128

Total Fat: 14.2g

    Saturated Fat: 8.3g

Cholesterol: 126mg

Sodium: 158mg

Potassium: 1230mg

Total Carbohydrates: 47.5g
    Dietary Fiber: 3g
    Sugar: 36.2g
Protein: 40.7g

32. Greek Yogurt Shake

Preparing time: 5 minutes
Servings: 6

1. Ingredients:

300g Greek Yogurt
100g coconut milk
2 tablespoon honey (30g)
40g raisin
200ml almond milk

2. Preparation:

Mix all ingredients in a blender until the composition is smooth.

3. Nutritional facts (amount per 100g/entire composition):

Contains Vitamin A, C, iron, calcium.

Calories: 167	Potassium: 220mg
Calories from Fat: 101	Total Carbohydrates: 13.6g
Total Fat: 11.2g	Dietary Fiber: 1.2g
Saturated Fat: 9.8g	Sugar: 11.5g
	Protein: 5.5g
Cholesterol: 2mg	Calories: 1169
Sodium: 21mg	Calories from Fat: 706

Total Fat: 78.4g

   Saturated Fat: 68.5g

Cholesterol: 15mg

Sodium: 149mg

Potassium: 1541mg

Total Carbohydrates: 95.1g
   Dietary Fiber: 8.2g
   Sugar: 80.3g

Protein: 38.3g

33. Coffee & Banana Shake

Preparing time: 5 minutes
Servings: 6

1. Ingredients:

25g coffee (grinder)
2 bananas
150ml almond milk
20g peanut butter
100ml water
5 eggs

2. Preparation:

Mix all ingredients in a blender until the composition is smooth.

3. Nutritional facts (amount per 100g/entire composition):

Contains Vitamin A, C, iron, calcium.

Calories: 142

    Calories from Fat: 89

Total Fat: 9.9g

    Saturated Fat: 5.9g

Cholesterol: 117mg

Sodium: 61mg

Potassium: 240mg

Total Carbohydrates: 9.7g

    Dietary Fiber: 1.5g

    Sugar: 5.4g

Protein: 5.5g

Calories: 992

    Calories from Fat: 621

Total Fat: 69g

    Saturated Fat: 41.4g

Cholesterol: 818mg

Sodium: 429mg

Potassium: 1683mg

Total Carbohydrates: 68g
    Dietary Fiber: 10.7g
    Sugar: 37.5g

Protein: 38.8g

34. Spinach Shake

Preparing time: 5 minutes
Servings: 7

1. Ingredients:

200g spinach
50g parsley
70g raspberries
200ml milk
100ml water
50g sour cream
50g whey protein

2. Preparation:

Mix all ingredients in a blender until the composition is smooth.

3. Nutritional facts (amount per 100g/entire composition):

Contains Vitamin A, C, iron, calcium.

Calories: 72

Calories from Fat: 25

Total Fat: 2.8g

Saturated Fat: 1.5g

Cholesterol: 20mg

Sodium: 58mg

Potassium: 282mg

Total Carbohydrates: 5.3g
Dietary Fiber: 1.5g
Sugar: 2.2g
Protein: 7.4g
Calories: 504

Calories from Fat: 174

Total Fat: 19.3g

    Saturated Fat: 10.8g

Cholesterol: 143mg

Sodium: 403mg

Potassium: 1973mg

Total Carbohydrates: 37g
    Dietary Fiber: 10.6g
    Sugar: 15.2g

Protein: 52.1g

35. Chia Shake

Preparing time: 5 minutes
Servings: 5

1. Ingredients:

100g chia seeds
200ml almond milk
50 sour cream
50g parsley
100ml water
40g whey protein

2. Preparation:

Mix all ingredients in a blender until the composition is smooth.

3. Nutritional facts (amount per 100g/entire composition):

Contains Vitamin A, C, iron, calcium.

Calories: 174

    Calories from Fat: 123

Total Fat: 13.7g

    Saturated Fat: 10g

Cholesterol: 20mg

Sodium: 30mg

Potassium: 260mg

Total Carbohydrates: 6.2g
    Dietary Fiber: 3.3g
    Sugar: 1.7g

Protein: 8.4g
Calories: 872

    Calories from Fat: 615

Total Fat: 68.3g

    Saturated Fat: 50.1g

Cholesterol: 99mg

Sodium: 152mg

Potassium: 1300mg

Total Carbohydrates: 31.2g
    Dietary Fiber: 16.5g
    Sugar: 8.5g
Protein: 42.1g

36. Papaya Shake

Preparing time: 5 minutes
Servings: 6

1. Ingredients:

3 papaya fruits
50g oats
300ml milk
1 teaspoon vanillas extract
50g whey protein

2. Preparation:

Mix all ingredients in a blender until the composition is smooth.

3. Nutritional facts (amount per 100g/entire composition):

Contains Vitamin A, C, iron, calcium.

Calories: 95	Potassium: 81mg
Calories from Fat: 14	Total Carbohydrates: 14.1g
Total Fat: 1.6g	Dietary Fiber: 1.4g
Saturated Fat: 0.7g	Sugar: 5.4g
	Protein: 6.5g
Cholesterol: 16mg	Calories: 760
Sodium: 34mg	Calories from Fat: 113

Total Fat: 12.6g

    Saturated Fat: 5.9g

Cholesterol: 130mg

Sodium: 268mg

Potassium: 648mg

Total Carbohydrates: 113g
    Dietary Fiber: 11.1g
    Sugar: 43.5g
Protein: 52.4g

37. Vanilla & Avocado Shake

Preparing time: 5 minutes
Servings: 8

1. Ingredients:

3 avocados
20g vanilla sugar
150ml milk
200ml water
1 teaspoon vanilla extract
40g whey protein (vanilla)

2. Preparation:

Mix all ingredients in a blender until the composition is smooth.

3. Nutritional facts (amount per 100g/entire composition):

Contains Vitamin A, C, iron, calcium.

Calories: 155

Calories from Fat: 111

Total Fat: 12.3g

Saturated Fat: 2.8g

Cholesterol: 10mg

Sodium: 19mg

Potassium: 325mg

Total Carbohydrates: 8.5g
Dietary Fiber: 4g
Sugar: 3.2g
Protein: 4.5g
Calories: 1549

Calories from Fat: 1108

Homemade Protein Shakes for Maximum Muscle Growth

Total Fat: 123.1g

    Saturated Fat: 27.8g

Cholesterol: 96mg

Sodium: 187mg

Potassium: 3248mg

Total Carbohydrates: 84.8g
    Dietary Fiber: 40.4g
    Sugar: 31.7g
Protein: 45.1g

38. Cherry & Almonds Shake

Preparing time: 5 minutes
Servings: 8

1. Ingredients:

300g cherries
100g almond milk
6 eggs
30g almonds (chopped)
75g sour cream
200g milk
1 tablespoon vanillas extract

2. Preparation:

Mix all ingredients in a blender until the composition is smooth.

3. Nutritional facts (amount per 100g/entire composition):

Contains Vitamin A, C, iron, calcium.

Calories: 158	Sodium: 64mg
Calories from Fat: 85	Potassium: 155mg
Total Fat: 9.5g	Total Carbohydrates: 12.5g
Saturated Fat: 4.8g	Dietary Fiber: 0.9g
Cholesterol: 115mg	Sugar: 1.9g
	Protein: 5.8g

Homemade Protein Shakes for Maximum Muscle Growth

Calories: 1424

    Calories from Fat: 766

Total Fat: 85.1g

    Saturated Fat: 42.8g

Cholesterol: 1031mg

Sodium: 574mg

Potassium: 1394mg

Total Carbohydrates: 113g
    Dietary Fiber: 7.8g
    Sugar: 17.4g
Protein: 51.9g

39. Carrot Shake

Preparing time: 5 minutes
Servings: 8

1. Ingredients:

300g carrots
200g strawberries
30g parsley
200ml milk
50g coconut milk
30g oats
5 eggs

2. Preparation:

Mix all ingredients in a blender until the composition is smooth.

3. Nutritional facts (amount per 100g/entire composition):

Contains Vitamin A, C, iron, calcium.

Calories: 84

Calories from Fat: 37

Total Fat: 4.1g

Saturated Fat: 2g

Cholesterol: 84mg

Sodium: 64mg

Potassium: 208mg

Total Carbohydrates: 8.2g
Dietary Fiber: 1.7g
Sugar: 3.8g
Protein: 4.4g
Calories: 844

Calories from Fat: 367

Total Fat: 40.8g

   Saturated Fat: 20.3g

Cholesterol: 835mg

Sodium: 640mg

Potassium: 2085mg

Total Carbohydrates: 81.7g
   Dietary Fiber: 16.5g
   Sugar: 37.8g
Protein: 44.2g

40. Grape Shake

Preparing time: 5 minutes
Servings: 8

1. Ingredients:

400g grapes
50g blueberries
200ml milk
100g Greek Yogurt
1 tablespoon vanilla extract
50g whey protein

2. Preparation:

Mix all ingredients in a blender until the composition is smooth.

3. Nutritional facts (amount per 100g/entire composition):

Contains Vitamin A, C, iron, calcium.

Calories: 88	Potassium: 171mg
Calories from Fat: 12	Total Carbohydrates: 12.2g
Total Fat: 1.4g	Dietary Fiber: 0.6g
Saturated Fat: 0.8g	Sugar: 10.8g
	Protein: 6.9g
Cholesterol: 16mg	Calories: 706
Sodium: 29mg	Calories from Fat: 97

Homemade Protein Shakes for Maximum Muscle Growth

Total Fat: 10.8g

Saturated Fat: 6g

Cholesterol: 126mg

Sodium: 229mg

Potassium: 1364mg

Total Carbohydrates: 97.6g
Dietary Fiber: 4.8g
Sugar: 86.4g
Protein: 55.4g

41. Cashew and Cacao Shake

Preparing time: 5 minutes
Servings: 4

1. Ingredients:

50g cashew (chopped)
2 tablespoon cacao powder (30g)
100ml almond milk
200ml water
50g whey protein (chocolate)

2. Preparation:

Mix all ingredients in a blender until the composition is smooth.

3. Nutritional facts (amount per 100g/entire composition):

Contains Vitamin C, iron, calcium.

Calories: 197

    Calories from Fat: 127

Total Fat: 14.1g

    Saturated Fat: 7.8g

Cholesterol: 26mg

Sodium: 30mg

Potassium: 209mg

Total Carbohydrates: 10.7g
    Dietary Fiber: 3.2g
    Sugar: 1.9g
Protein: 12.9g
Calories: 789

    Calories from Fat: 507

Total Fat: 56.3g

    Saturated Fat: 31.3g

Cholesterol: 104mg

Sodium: 119mg

Potassium: 834mg

Total Carbohydrates: 42.9g
    Dietary Fiber: 12.7g
    Sugar: 7.4g
Protein: 51.7g

42. Kale Shake

Preparing time: 5 minutes
Servings: 6

1. Ingredients:

300g kale
50g parsley
1 lime (juice)
20g ginger
300ml water
50ml milk
50g whey protein

2. Preparation:

Mix all ingredients in a blender until the composition is smooth.

3. Nutritional facts (amount per 100g/entire composition):

Contains Vitamin A, C, iron, calcium.

Calories: 59	Sodium: 36mg
Calories from Fat: 6	Potassium: 300mg
Total Fat: 0.7g	Total Carbohydrates: 8g
Saturated Fat: 0g	Dietary Fiber: 1.3g
	Sugar: 0.8g
Cholesterol: 14mg	Protein: 6.3g
	Calories: 475

Calories from Fat: 52

Total Fat: 5.8g

   Saturated Fat: 2.6g

Cholesterol: 108mg

Sodium: 288mg

Potassium: 2402mg

Total Carbohydrates: 64.2g
   Dietary Fiber: 10.5g
   Sugar: 6g
Protein: 50.1g

43. Lettuce Shake

Preparing time: 5 minutes
Servings: 8

1. Ingredients:

300g lettuce
50g spinach
30g parsley
100ml almond milk
30g oats
5 eggs
300ml milk

2. Preparation:

Mix all ingredients in a blender until the composition is smooth.

3. Nutritional facts (amount per 100g/entire composition):

Contains Vitamin A, C, iron, calcium.

Calories: 88	Sodium: 54mg
Calories from Fat: 50	Potassium: 172mg
Total Fat: 5.5g	Total Carbohydrates: 5.6g
Saturated Fat: 3.2g	Dietary Fiber: 0.9g
	Sugar: 2.3g
Cholesterol: 84mg	Protein: 4.8g
	Calories: 880

Calories from Fat: 498

Total Fat: 55.3g

   Saturated Fat: 32.5g

Cholesterol: 844mg

Sodium: 544mg

Potassium: 1716mg

Total Carbohydrates: 55.6g
   Dietary Fiber: 9.3g
   Sugar: 22.8g
Protein: 47.8g

44. Kale & Ginger Shake

Preparing time: 5 minutes
Servings: 6

1. Ingredients:

200g kale
20g ginger
4 eggs
50g coconut milk
100g Greek yogurt
200g almond milk
1-2 tablespoon honey (15-30g)
20g chia seeds

2. Preparation:

Mix all ingredients in a blender until the composition is smooth.

3. Nutritional facts (amount per 100g/entire composition):

Contains Vitamin A, C, iron, calcium.

Calories: 146	Cholesterol: 82mg
Calories from Fat: 93	Sodium: 51mg
Total Fat: 10.3g	Potassium: 292mg
Saturated Fat: 7.6g	Total Carbohydrates: 9.2g
	Dietary Fiber: 1.6g

Sugar: 4g
Protein: 5.9g
Calories: 1165

Calories from Fat: 740

Total Fat: 82.2g

Saturated Fat: 60.4g

Cholesterol: 660mg

Sodium: 410mg

Potassium: 2338mg

Total Carbohydrates: 73.7g
Dietary Fiber: 13.1g
Sugar: 31.6g
Protein: 47g

45. Cucumber Shake

Preparing time: 5 minutes
Servings: 6

1. Ingredients:

300g cucumber
50g parsley
80g cottage cheese
1 teaspoon lime extract (5g)
300ml water
40g whey protein

2. Preparation:

Mix all ingredients in a blender until the composition is smooth.

3. Nutritional facts (amount per 100g/entire composition):

Contains Vitamin A, C, iron, calcium.

Calories: 39	Potassium: 137mg
Calories from Fat: 5	Total Carbohydrates: 3.6g
	Dietary Fiber: 0.6g
Total Fat: 0.6g	Sugar: 1g
Saturated Fat: 0g	Protein: 5.4g
	Calories: 310
Cholesterol: 11mg	
	Calories from Fat: 43
Sodium: 55mg	

Total Fat: 4.8g

    Saturated Fat: 2.4g

Cholesterol: 90mg

Sodium: 441mg

Potassium: 1092mg

Total Carbohydrates: 28.8g
Dietary Fiber: 5g
Sugar: 8g
Protein: 43.5g

46. Matcha Shake

Preparing time: 5 minutes
Servings: 6

1. Ingredients:

20g matcha
1 lime (juice)
100g Greek yogurt
5 eggs
50g parsley
50ml coconut milk
200ml milk

2. Preparation:

Mix all ingredients in a blender until the composition is smooth.

3. Nutritional facts (amount per 100g/entire composition):

Contains Vitamin A, C, iron, calcium.

Calories: 94	Sodium: 68mg
Calories from Fat: 52	Potassium: 148mg
Total Fat: 5.8g	Total Carbohydrates: 4.6g
Saturated Fat: 3.1g	Dietary Fiber: 0.7g
	Sugar: 3g
Cholesterol: 120mg	Protein: 6.8g
	Calories: 661

Calories from Fat: 367

Total Fat: 40.8g

   Saturated Fat: 21.7g

Cholesterol: 840mg

Sodium: 477mg

Potassium: 1033mg

Total Carbohydrates: 32.1g
   Dietary Fiber: 4.7g
   Sugar: 21.3g
Protein: 47.6g

47. Broccoli Shake

Preparing time: 5 minutes
Servings: 6

1. Ingredients:

200g broccoli
50g parsley
30g spinach
30g cottage cheese
300ml milk
100ml water
4 eggs

2. Preparation:

Mix all ingredients in a blender until the composition is smooth.

3. Nutritional facts (amount per 100g/entire composition):

Contains Vitamin A, C, iron, calcium.

Calories: 59

Calories from Fat: 25

Total Fat: 2.8g

Saturated Fat: 1.1g

Cholesterol: 76mg

Sodium: 71mg

Potassium: 169mg

Total Carbohydrates: 3.9g
Dietary Fiber: 0.8g
Sugar: 2.1g
Protein: 4.9g
Calories: 526

Calories from Fat: 230

Total Fat: 25.6g

Saturated Fat: 9.7g

Cholesterol: 682mg

Sodium: 635mg

Potassium: 1521mg

Total Carbohydrates: 35.2g
Dietary Fiber: 7.5g
Sugar: 19.4g
Protein: 44.4g

48. Kale & Banana Shake

Preparing time: 5 minutes
Servings: 6

1. Ingredients:

150ml coconut milk
70g kale
30g spinach
1 banana
40g whey protein
200ml water
Sweetener per taste (honey/brown sugar)

2. Preparation:

Mix all ingredients in a blender until the composition is smooth.

3. Nutritional facts (amount per 100g/entire composition):

Contains Vitamin A, C, iron, calcium.

Calories: 109	Sodium: 26mg
Calories from Fat: 59	Potassium: 260mg
Total Fat: 6.5g	Total Carbohydrates: 8.1g
Saturated Fat: 5.6g	Dietary Fiber: 1.4g
	Sugar: 3.5g
Cholesterol: 14mg	Protein: 6g
	Calories: 651

Calories from Fat: 352

Total Fat: 39.2g

   Saturated Fat: 33.5g

Cholesterol: 83mg

Sodium: 155mg

Potassium: 1562mg

Total Carbohydrates: 48.5g
   Dietary Fiber: 8.1g
   Sugar: 20.8g
Protein: 36.3g

49. Mango & Peach Shake

Preparing time: 5 minutes
Servings: 8

1. Ingredients:

2 mango fruits
4-6 peaches
300ml milk
50g Greek yogurt
40g whey protein

2. Preparation:

Mix all ingredients in a blender until the composition is smooth.

3. Nutritional facts (amount per 100g/entire composition):

Contains Vitamin A, C, iron, calcium.

Calories: 64

Calories from Fat: 10

Total Fat: 1.1g

Saturated Fat: 0.6g

Cholesterol: 11mg

Sodium: 24mg

Potassium: 153mg

Total Carbohydrates: 9.3g
Dietary Fiber: 0.9g
Sugar: 8g

Protein: 4.8g
Calories: 640

Calories from Fat: 101

Total Fat: 11.2g

Saturated Fat: 5.9g

Cholesterol: 111mg

Sodium: 238mg

Potassium: 1531mg

Total Carbohydrates: 93.4g
Dietary Fiber: 9.5g
Sugar: 80g
Protein: 48.3g

50. Green Shake

Preparing time: 5 minutes
Servings: 6

1. Ingredients:

100g parsley
200g kale
100g raspberries
1 teaspoon lime extract (5g)
200ml water
30ml milk
60g whey protein

2. Preparation:

Mix all ingredients in a blender until the composition is smooth.

3. Nutritional facts (amount per 100g/entire composition):

Contains Vitamin A, C, iron, calcium.

Calories: 62

Calories from Fat: 7

Total Fat: 0.8g

Saturated Fat: 0g

Cholesterol: 18mg

Sodium: 39mg

Potassium: 292mg

Total Carbohydrates: 6.8g
Dietary Fiber: 1.8g
Sugar: 1.2g
Protein: 7.7g
Calories: 435

Calories from Fat: 51

Total Fat: 5.6g

    Saturated Fat: 2.3g

Cholesterol: 128mg

Sodium: 271mg

Potassium: 2046mg

Total Carbohydrates: 47.9g
    Dietary Fiber: 12.8g
    Sugar: 8.4g
Protein: 54g

51. Guava Shake

Preparing time: 5 minutes
Servings: 6

1. Ingredients:

2 guava fruits
6 eggs
200ml milk
20ml coconut milk
20ml almond milk
1 teaspoon vanillas extract (5g)
Sweetener per taste (honey/brown sugar)

2. Preparation:

Mix all ingredients in a blender until the composition is smooth.

3. Nutritional facts (amount per 100g/entire composition):

Contains Vitamin A, C, iron, calcium.

Calories: 101	Sodium: 68mg
Calories from Fat: 54	Potassium: 191mg
Total Fat: 6g	Total Carbohydrates: 5.8g
Saturated Fat: 2.8g	Dietary Fiber: 1.5g
	Sugar: 4.2g
Cholesterol: 143mg	Protein: 6.5g
	Calories: 709

Homemade Protein Shakes for Maximum Muscle Growth

Calories from Fat: 377

Total Fat: 41.9g

    Saturated Fat: 19.8g

Cholesterol: 999mg

Sodium: 477mg

Potassium: 1336mg

Total Carbohydrates: 40.7g
    Dietary Fiber: 10.6g
    Sugar: 29.3g
Protein: 45.5g

52. Mulberries Shake

Preparing time: 5 minutes
Servings: 6

1. Ingredients:

300g mulberries
200g spinach
50g cottage cheese
300g milk
3 eggs
30g oats

2. Preparation:

Mix all ingredients in a blender until the composition is smooth.

3. Nutritional facts (amount per 100g/entire composition):

Contains Vitamin A, C, iron, calcium.

Calories: 67

Calories from Fat: 22

Total Fat: 2.4g

Saturated Fat: 0.9g

Cholesterol: 52mg

Sodium: 72mg

Potassium: 220mg

Total Carbohydrates: 7.5g
Dietary Fiber: 1.2g
Sugar: 4g

Protein: 4.7g
Calories: 672

Calories from Fat: 217

Total Fat: 24.1g

    Saturated Fat: 8.9g

Cholesterol: 520mg

Sodium: 719mg

Potassium: 2204mg

Total Carbohydrates: 74.6g
    Dietary Fiber: 12.5g
    Sugar: 40.1g
Protein: 47.3g

53. Grapefruits Shake

Preparing time: 5 minutes
Servings: 6

1. Ingredients:

2 grapefruits
200g Greek yogurt
200ml water
30g sweetener (honey/brown sugar)
50g whey protein

2. Preparation:

Mix all ingredients in a blender until the composition is smooth.

3. Nutritional facts (amount per 100g/entire composition):

Contains Vitamin A, C, iron, calcium.

Calories: 61	Potassium: 132mg
Calories from Fat: 9	Total Carbohydrates: 10g
	Dietary Fiber: 2.9g
Total Fat: 1g	Sugar: 3.9g
	Protein: 8.2g
Saturated Fat: 0.7g	Calories: 425
Cholesterol: 16mg	Calories from Fat: 65
Sodium: 23mg	Total Fat: 7.2g

Saturated Fat: 4.5g

Cholesterol: 114mg

Sodium: 160mg

Potassium: 923mg

Total Carbohydrates: 69.9g
Dietary Fiber: 20.5g
Sugar: 27.4g
Protein: 57.3g

54. Melon Shake

Preparing time: 5 minutes
Servings: 6

1. Ingredients:

300g melon
200g Greek Yogurt
100ml water
20g sweetener (honey/brown sugar)
50g whey protein

2. Preparation:

Mix all ingredients in a blender until the composition is smooth.

3. Nutritional facts (amount per 100g/entire composition):

Contains Vitamin A, C, iron, calcium.

Calories: 64

Calories from Fat: 10

Total Fat: 1.1g

Saturated Fat: 0.7g

Cholesterol: 16mg

Sodium: 29mg

Potassium: 195mg

Total Carbohydrates: 8.8g
Dietary Fiber: 2.1g
Sugar: 4.7g

Protein: 8.3g
Calories: 445

Calories from Fat: 68

Total Fat: 7.6g

Saturated Fat: 4.6g

Cholesterol: 114mg

Sodium: 205mg

Potassium: 1367mg

Total Carbohydrates: 62g
  Dietary Fiber: 14.5g
  Sugar: 33.1g
Protein: 58.2g

55. Pomegranate Shake

Preparing time: 5 minutes
Servings: 6

1. Ingredients:

4 pomegranates
60g whey powder
200ml milk
1 teaspoon vanilla extract
20g sour cream

2. Preparation:

Mix all ingredients in a blender until the composition is smooth.

3. Nutritional facts (amount per 100g/entire composition):

Contains Vitamin A, C, iron, calcium.

Calories: 88	Potassium: 233mg
Calories from Fat: 12	Total Carbohydrates: 13.6g
Total Fat: 1.3g	Dietary Fiber: 0g
Saturated Fat: 0.8g	Sugar: 10.6g
	Protein: 6g
Cholesterol: 17mg	Calories: 790
Sodium: 24mg	Calories from Fat: 108

Homemade Protein Shakes for Maximum Muscle Growth

Total Fat: 12g

    Saturated Fat: 6.9g

Cholesterol: 151mg

Sodium: 215mg

Potassium: 2093mg

Total Carbohydrates: 123g
Dietary Fiber: 4g
Sugar: 95.7g
Protein: 54.2g

56. Kiwi Shake

Preparing time: 5 minutes
Servings: 6

1. Ingredients:

100g kiwis
8 eggs
200ml milk
20g sweetener (honey/brown sugar)
100g Greek yogurt

2. Preparation:

Mix all ingredients in a blender until the composition is smooth.

3. Nutritional facts (amount per 100g/entire composition):

Contains Vitamin A, C, iron, calcium.

Calories: 93

Calories from Fat: 47

Total Fat: 5.2g

Saturated Fat: 1.9g

Cholesterol: 166mg

Sodium: 78mg

Potassium: 130mg

Total Carbohydrates: 6.9g
Dietary Fiber: 1.9g
Sugar: 3.1g

Protein: 7.8g
Calories: 743

Calories from Fat: 376

Total Fat: 41.7g

Saturated Fat: 15g

Cholesterol: 1331mg

Sodium: 626mg

Potassium: 1043mg

Total Carbohydrates: 55g
    Dietary Fiber: 14.8g
    Sugar: 25g
Protein: 62.2g

57. Kiwi & Strawberry Shake

Preparing time: 5 minutes
Servings: 6

1. Ingredients:

200g kiwis
150g strawberries
50g Greek yogurt
200ml milk
60g whey powder

2. Preparation:

Mix all ingredients in a blender until the composition is smooth.

3. Nutritional facts (amount per 100g/entire composition):

Contains Vitamin A, C, iron, calcium.

Calories: 78

Calories from Fat: 13

Total Fat: 1.5g

Saturated Fat: 0.7g

Cholesterol: 21mg

Sodium: 33mg

Potassium: 197mg

Total Carbohydrates: 8.6g
Dietary Fiber: 1.3g
Sugar: 5.5g

Protein: 8.3g

Calories: 543

Calories from Fat: 93

Total Fat: 10.3g

Saturated Fat: 5.1g

Cholesterol: 144mg

Sodium: 228mg

Potassium: 1382mg

Total Carbohydrates: 60.1g
Dietary Fiber: 9g
Sugar: 38.4g
Protein: 57.9g

58. Cantaloupe Melon Shake

Preparing time: 5 minutes
Servings: 6

1. Ingredients:

1 cantaloupe melon (500g)
200g Greek yogurt
1 teaspoon vanilla extract (5g)
100ml milk
40g oats
6 eggs

2. Preparation:

Mix all ingredients in a blender until the composition is smooth.

3. Nutritional facts (amount per 100g/entire composition):

Contains Vitamin A, C, iron, calcium.

Calories: 111

Calories from Fat: 45

Total Fat: 5g

Saturated Fat: 1.8g

Cholesterol: 143mg

Sodium: 72mg

Potassium: 121mg

Total Carbohydrates: 7.2g
Dietary Fiber: 0.7g
Sugar: 3.2g

Protein: 9g
Calories: 775

Calories from Fat: 315

Total Fat: 35g

Saturated Fat: 12.9g

Cholesterol: 1001mg

Sodium: 502mg

Potassium: 846mg

Total Carbohydrates: 50.7g
Dietary Fiber: 5g
Sugar: 22.6g
Protein: 62.9g

59. Passion Fruit Shake

Preparing time: 5 minutes
Servings: 4

1. Ingredients:

6 passion fruits (peal)
50g strawberries
200ml almond milk
50ml milk
1 teaspoon vanilla extract (5g)
60g whey protein

2. Preparation:

Mix all ingredients in a blender until the composition is smooth.

3. Nutritional facts (amount per 100g/entire composition):

Contains Vitamin A, C, iron, calcium.

Calories: 171

Calories from Fat: 97

Total Fat: 10.8g

Saturated Fat: 9.1g

Cholesterol: 26mg

Sodium: 39mg

Potassium: 272mg

Total Carbohydrates: 10.1g
Dietary Fiber: 3.3g
Sugar: 5.2g
Protein: 10.4g
Calories: 857

Calories from Fat: 485

Homemade Protein Shakes for Maximum Muscle Growth

Total Fat: 53.9g

   Saturated Fat: 45.4g

Cholesterol: 129mg

Sodium: 193mg

Potassium: 1361mg

Total Carbohydrates: 50.5g
   Dietary Fiber: 16.7g
   Sugar: 26g
Protein: 51.9g

60. Currants Shake

Preparing time: 5 minutes
Servings: 6

1. Ingredients:

350g currant
200ml milk
1 teaspoon peanut butter (15g)
7 eggs
100g Greek Yogurt

2. Preparation:

Mix all ingredients in a blender until the composition is smooth.

3. Nutritional facts (amount per 100g/entire composition):

Contains Vitamin A, C, iron, calcium.

Calories: 85

Calories from Fat: 36

Total Fat: 4g

Saturated Fat: 1.4g

Cholesterol: 117mg

Sodium: 59mg

Potassium: 167mg

Total Carbohydrates: 6.6g
Dietary Fiber: 1.5g
Sugar: 4.2g

Protein: 6.2g
Calories: 846

Calories from Fat: 326

Total Fat: 40.2g

Saturated Fat: 14.2g

Cholesterol: 1168mg

Sodium: 589mg

Potassium: 1669mg

Total Carbohydrates: 65.9g
Dietary Fiber: 15.4g
Sugar: 42g
Protein: 61.7g

OTHER GREAT TITLES BY THIS AUTHOR

www.ingramcontent.com/pod-product-compliance
Lightning Source LLC
Chambersburg PA
CBHW071739080526
44588CB00013B/2087